VAN LIVING:

OUR DAY-BY-DAY ADVENTURE

KRISTINE HUDSON

© 2020 Van Living: Our Day-By-Day Adventure

All rights reserved. No part of the book may be reproduced in any shape or form without permission from the publisher.

This guide is written from a combination of experience and high-level research. Even though we have done our best to ensure this book is accurate and up to date, there are no guarantees to the accuracy or completeness of the contents herein.

This cover has been designed using resources from freepik.com

ISBN: 978-1-953714-37-4

"A good traveler has no fixed plans and is not intent on arriving."
— Lao Tzu

CHECKLIST

- [ ] PASSPORT
- [ ] LONGER WORDS WILL FIT
- [ ] LONGER WORDS WILL FIT HERE
- [ ] PASSPORT
- [ ] LONGER WORDS WILL FIT
- [ ] LONGER WORDS WILL FIT HERE
- [ ] PASSPORT
- [ ] LONGER WORDS WILL FIT
- [ ] LONGER WORDS WILL FIT HERE
- [ ] PASSPORT
- [ ] LONGER WORDS WILL FIT
- [ ] LONGER WORDS WILL FIT HERE
- [ ] PASSPORT
- [ ] LONGER WORDS WILL FIT
- [ ] LONGER WORDS WILL FIT HERE
- [ ] PASSPORT
- [ ] LONGER WORDS WILL FIT
- [ ] LONGER WORDS WILL FIT HERE
- [ ] PASSPORT
- [ ] LONGER WORDS WILL FIT
- [ ] LONGER WORDS WILL FIT HERE
- [ ] PASSPORT
- [ ] LONGER WORDS WILL FIT
- [ ] LONGER WORDS WILL FIT HERE
- [ ] LONGER WORDS WILL FIT
- [ ] LONGER WORDS WILL FIT HERE
- [ ] PASSPORT
- [ ] LONGER WORDS WILL FIT
- [ ] LONGER WORDS WILL FIT HERE
- [ ] LONGER WORDS WILL FIT HERE

- [ ] PASSPORT
- [ ] LONGER WORDS WILL FIT
- [ ] LONGER WORDS WILL FIT HERE
- [ ] PASSPORT
- [ ] LONGER WORDS WILL FIT
- [ ] LONGER WORDS WILL FIT HERE
- [ ] PASSPORT
- [ ] LONGER WORDS WILL FIT
- [ ] LONGER WORDS WILL FIT HERE
- [ ] PASSPORT
- [ ] LONGER WORDS WILL FIT
- [ ] LONGER WORDS WILL FIT HERE
- [ ] PASSPORT
- [ ] LONGER WORDS WILL FIT
- [ ] LONGER WORDS WILL FIT HERE
- [ ] PASSPORT
- [ ] LONGER WORDS WILL FIT
- [ ] LONGER WORDS WILL FIT HERE
- [ ] PASSPORT
- [ ] LONGER WORDS WILL FIT
- [ ] LONGER WORDS WILL FIT HERE
- [ ] PASSPORT
- [ ] LONGER WORDS WILL FIT
- [ ] LONGER WORDS WILL FIT HERE
- [ ] LONGER WORDS WILL FIT
- [ ] LONGER WORDS WILL FIT HERE
- [ ] PASSPORT
- [ ] LONGER WORDS WILL FIT
- [ ] LONGER WORDS WILL FIT HERE
- [ ] LONGER WORDS WILL FIT HERE

- [ ] PASSPORT
- [ ] LONGER WORDS WILL FIT
- [ ] LONGER WORDS WILL FIT HERE
- [ ] PASSPORT
- [ ] LONGER WORDS WILL FIT
- [ ] LONGER WORDS WILL FIT HERE
- [ ] PASSPORT
- [ ] LONGER WORDS WILL FIT
- [ ] LONGER WORDS WILL FIT HERE
- [ ] PASSPORT
- [ ] LONGER WORDS WILL FIT
- [ ] LONGER WORDS WILL FIT HERE
- [ ] PASSPORT
- [ ] LONGER WORDS WILL FIT
- [ ] LONGER WORDS WILL FIT HERE
- [ ] PASSPORT
- [ ] LONGER WORDS WILL FIT
- [ ] LONGER WORDS WILL FIT HERE
- [ ] PASSPORT
- [ ] LONGER WORDS WILL FIT
- [ ] LONGER WORDS WILL FIT HERE
- [ ] LONGER WORDS WILL FIT
- [ ] LONGER WORDS WILL FIT HERE
- [ ] PASSPORT
- [ ] LONGER WORDS WILL FIT
- [ ] LONGER WORDS WILL FIT HERE
- [ ] LONGER WORDS WILL FIT HERE

- [ ] PASSPORT
- [ ] LONGER WORDS WILL FIT
- [ ] LONGER WORDS WILL FIT HERE
- [ ] PASSPORT
- [ ] LONGER WORDS WILL FIT
- [ ] LONGER WORDS WILL FIT HERE
- [ ] PASSPORT
- [ ] LONGER WORDS WILL FIT
- [ ] LONGER WORDS WILL FIT HERE
- [ ] PASSPORT
- [ ] LONGER WORDS WILL FIT
- [ ] LONGER WORDS WILL FIT HERE
- [ ] PASSPORT
- [ ] LONGER WORDS WILL FIT
- [ ] LONGER WORDS WILL FIT HERE
- [ ] PASSPORT
- [ ] LONGER WORDS WILL FIT
- [ ] LONGER WORDS WILL FIT HERE
- [ ] PASSPORT
- [ ] LONGER WORDS WILL FIT
- [ ] LONGER WORDS WILL FIT HERE
- [ ] LONGER WORDS WILL FIT
- [ ] LONGER WORDS WILL FIT HERE
- [ ] _____
- [ ] _____
- [ ] _____
- [ ] _____

DATE: ___ / ___ / ___

GOALS:

_____
_____
_____
_____
_____

LOCATIONS VISITED:

_____
_____
_____
_____
_____

THE TOP THREE MEMORIES:

1. _____
2. _____
3. _____

Many people seek Van Life because of the promises of a non-traditional lifestyle, in which you're free to explore, move around as you wish, and live unattached to societal norms. How do those concepts relate to you and the choices you've made in your van lifestyle? Are you feeling disconnected with reality, or more connected to your own existence than ever before? Use this space to reflect upon and celebrate your own feelings of independence.

_____
_____
_____
_____
_____
_____
_____
_____
_____
_____
_____
_____
_____
_____
_____
_____
_____
_____
_____
_____

DATE: ___ / ___ / ___

NAME: _____

OUR ADVENTURE BEGINS: _____

OUR POINT OF ORIGIN IS: _____

TODAY'S DESTINATION: _____

TODAY'S PASSENGER LOG:

_____
_____
_____
_____
_____

WE SPENT THE NIGHT AT:

_____
_____

THE BEST PART OF THE DAY WAS:

_____
_____
_____
_____

TODAY'S LESSON/THINGS WE LEARNED:

_____
_____
_____
_____

TODAY'S CAMPFIRE MENU:

Today's writing prompt is a word. Take a few moments to meditate on this word, then write about how it relates to you and your adventures so far.

Balance

DATE: ___ / ___ / ___

NAME: _____

OUR ADVENTURE BEGINS: _____

OUR POINT OF ORIGIN IS: _____

TODAY'S DESTINATION: _____

TODAY'S PASSENGER LOG:
_____
_____
_____
_____

WE SPENT THE NIGHT AT:
_____
_____

THE BEST PART OF THE DAY WAS:
_____
_____
_____
_____

TODAY'S LESSON/THINGS WE LEARNED:
_____
_____
_____
_____

TODAY'S CAMPFIRE MENU:

Free Write:

Here is your chance to write what is on your mind, in your heart, or taking up space in your soul. Even if you don't think you have anything to write about today, take at least five minutes to free-form write whatever comes to mind. You might just be surprised!

DATE: ___ / ___ / ___

NAME: _____

OUR ADVENTURE BEGINS: _____

OUR POINT OF ORIGIN IS: _____

TODAY'S DESTINATION: _____

TODAY'S PASSENGER LOG:

_____
_____
_____
_____

WE SPENT THE NIGHT AT:

_____
_____

THE BEST PART OF THE DAY WAS:

_____
_____
_____
_____

TODAY'S LESSON/THINGS WE LEARNED:

_____
_____
_____
_____

TODAY'S CAMPFIRE MENU:

_____
_____
_____

A Letter to Pre-Van Life You:

Today's exercise is to explore how far you have come in your journeys. Take a few moments to write a letter to a past version of yourself to share all of the things you have learned so far. You can write to yourself as a child, as a teenager, or even take some time to share the fascinating things you've learned in just the past week.

At the end of the year, you'll be able to look back on all of the progress you have made as an individual, so don't be afraid to make note of both positive and negative experiences and emotions here.

_____
_____
_____
_____
_____
_____
_____
_____
_____
_____
_____
_____
_____
_____
_____
_____
_____
_____
_____

DATE: ___ / ___ / ___

NAME: _____

OUR ADVENTURE BEGINS: _____

OUR POINT OF ORIGIN IS: _____

TODAY'S DESTINATION: _____

TODAY'S PASSENGER LOG:
_____
_____
_____
_____

WE SPENT THE NIGHT AT:
_____
_____

THE BEST PART OF THE DAY WAS:
_____
_____
_____
_____

TODAY'S LESSON/THINGS WE LEARNED:
_____
_____
_____
_____

TODAY'S CAMPFIRE MENU:

Try something new today! Whether it's a new yoga pose, a different flavor of coffee, or exploring a National Park, do something out of the norm today.

DATE: ___ / ___ / ___

NAME:

OUR ADVENTURE BEGINS:

OUR POINT OF ORIGIN IS:

TODAY'S DESTINATION:

TODAY'S PASSENGER LOG:

WE SPENT THE NIGHT AT:

THE BEST PART OF THE DAY WAS:

TODAY'S LESSON/THINGS WE LEARNED:

TODAY'S CAMPFIRE MENU:

What's next? What are some things that you'd like to accomplish, now that you know you can make a go of this whole "van life" thing?

DATE: ___ / ___ / ___

NAME: _____

OUR ADVENTURE BEGINS: _____

OUR POINT OF ORIGIN IS: _____

TODAY'S DESTINATION: _____

TODAY'S PASSENGER LOG:

_____
_____
_____
_____

WE SPENT THE NIGHT AT:

_____
_____

THE BEST PART OF THE DAY WAS:

_____
_____
_____
_____

TODAY'S LESSON/THINGS WE LEARNED:

_____
_____
_____
_____

TODAY'S CAMPFIRE MENU:

"The best teacher is experience and not through someone's distorted point of view"
— Jack Kerouac

When you read this line, what comes to mind? Where are you in your adventure today? Reflect on this quote, and write your thoughts on how these words relate to your own journey.

DATE: ___ / ___ / ___

NAME:

OUR ADVENTURE BEGINS:

OUR POINT OF ORIGIN IS:

TODAY'S DESTINATION:

TODAY'S PASSENGER LOG:

WE SPENT THE NIGHT AT:

THE BEST PART OF THE DAY WAS:

TODAY'S LESSON/THINGS WE LEARNED:

TODAY'S CAMPFIRE MENU:

Each week, allow yourself some time to pause to reflect on the past week, and to set the intention for the new week.

Where have you been in the past week- in your travels, in your daily life? How have you felt, mentally and physically? How do you intend to change this in the coming week?

DATE: ___ / ___ / ___

NAME: _____

OUR ADVENTURE BEGINS: _____

OUR POINT OF ORIGIN IS: _____

TODAY'S DESTINATION: _____

TODAY'S PASSENGER LOG:
_____
_____
_____
_____

WE SPENT THE NIGHT AT:
_____
_____

THE BEST PART OF THE DAY WAS:
_____
_____
_____
_____

TODAY'S LESSON/THINGS WE LEARNED:
_____
_____
_____
_____

TODAY'S CAMPFIRE MENU:

Today's writing prompt is a word. Take a few moments to meditate on this word, then write about how it relates to you and your adventures so far.

Discovery

DATE: ___ / ___ / ___

NAME: _____

OUR ADVENTURE BEGINS: _____

OUR POINT OF ORIGIN IS: _____

TODAY'S DESTINATION: _____

TODAY'S PASSENGER LOG:
_____
_____
_____
_____

WE SPENT THE NIGHT AT:
_____
_____

THE BEST PART OF THE DAY WAS:
_____
_____
_____
_____

TODAY'S LESSON/THINGS WE LEARNED:
_____
_____
_____
_____

TODAY'S CAMPFIRE MENU:

Free Write:

Here is your chance to write what is on your mind, in your heart, or taking up space in your soul. Even if you don't think you have anything to write about today, take at least five minutes to free-form write whatever comes to mind. You might just be surprised!

DATE: ___ / ___ / ___

NAME: _____

OUR ADVENTURE BEGINS: _____

OUR POINT OF ORIGIN IS: _____

TODAY'S DESTINATION: _____

TODAY'S PASSENGER LOG:
_____
_____
_____
_____

WE SPENT THE NIGHT AT:
_____
_____

THE BEST PART OF THE DAY WAS:
_____
_____
_____
_____

TODAY'S LESSON/THINGS WE LEARNED:
_____
_____
_____
_____

TODAY'S CAMPFIRE MENU:

A Letter to Pre-Van Life You:

Today's exercise is to explore how far you have come in your journeys. Take a few moments to write a letter to a past version of yourself to share all of the things you have learned so far. You can write to yourself as a child, as a teenager, or even take some time to share the fascinating things you've learned in just the past week.

At the end of the year, you'll be able to look back on all of the progress you have made as an individual, so don't be afraid to make note of both positive and negative experiences and emotions here.

DATE: ___ / ___ / ___

NAME: _____

OUR ADVENTURE BEGINS: _____

OUR POINT OF ORIGIN IS: _____

TODAY'S DESTINATION: _____

TODAY'S PASSENGER LOG:

_____
_____
_____
_____

WE SPENT THE NIGHT AT:

_____
_____

THE BEST PART OF THE DAY WAS:

_____
_____
_____
_____

TODAY'S LESSON/THINGS WE LEARNED:

_____
_____
_____
_____

TODAY'S CAMPFIRE MENU:

How do you honestly feel about van life today? It's ok to have lots of different feelings, so use this time to explore your thoughts.

DATE: ___ / ___ / ___

NAME: _____

OUR ADVENTURE BEGINS: _____

OUR POINT OF ORIGIN IS: _____

TODAY'S DESTINATION: _____

TODAY'S PASSENGER LOG:
_____
_____
_____
_____

WE SPENT THE NIGHT AT:
_____
_____

THE BEST PART OF THE DAY WAS:
_____
_____
_____
_____

TODAY'S LESSON/THINGS WE LEARNED:
_____
_____
_____
_____

TODAY'S CAMPFIRE MENU:

Write about your worst day so far on this adventure. What went wrong? How did you feel? One day, you'll look back at this in a different light, so be sure to capture all of your thoughts and feelings.

DATE: ___ / ___ / ___

NAME:

OUR ADVENTURE BEGINS:

OUR POINT OF ORIGIN IS:

TODAY'S DESTINATION:

TODAY'S PASSENGER LOG:

WE SPENT THE NIGHT AT:

THE BEST PART OF THE DAY WAS:

TODAY'S LESSON/THINGS WE LEARNED:

TODAY'S CAMPFIRE MENU:

The journey changes you; it should change you. It leaves marks on your memory, on your consciousness, on your heart, and on your body. You take something with you. Hopefully, you leave something good behind
— **Anthony Bourdain**

When you read this line, what comes to mind? Where are you in your adventure today? Reflect on this quote, and write your thoughts on how these words relate to your own journey.

DATE: ___ / ___ / ___

NAME: _____

OUR ADVENTURE BEGINS: _____

OUR POINT OF ORIGIN IS: _____

TODAY'S DESTINATION: _____

TODAY'S PASSENGER LOG:

_____
_____
_____
_____

WE SPENT THE NIGHT AT:

_____
_____

THE BEST PART OF THE DAY WAS:

_____
_____
_____
_____

TODAY'S LESSON/THINGS WE LEARNED:

_____
_____
_____
_____

TODAY'S CAMPFIRE MENU:

_____
_____
_____

Each week, allow yourself some time to pause to reflect on the past week, and to set the intention for the new week.

Where have you been in the past week- in your travels, in your daily life? How have you felt, mentally and physically? How do you intend to change this in the coming week?

DATE: ___ / ___ / ___

NAME:

OUR ADVENTURE BEGINS:

OUR POINT OF ORIGIN IS:

TODAY'S DESTINATION:

TODAY'S PASSENGER LOG:

WE SPENT THE NIGHT AT:

THE BEST PART OF THE DAY WAS:

TODAY'S LESSON/THINGS WE LEARNED:

TODAY'S CAMPFIRE MENU:

Today's writing prompt is a word. Take a few moments to meditate on this word, then write about how it relates to you and your adventures so far.

Firmness

DAY 6 ___ / ___ / ___

NAME:

OUR ADVENTURE BEGINS:

OUR POINT OF ORIGIN IS:

TODAY'S DESTINATION:

TODAY'S PASSENGER LOG:

WE SPENT THE NIGHT AT:

THE BEST PART OF THE DAY WAS:

TODAY'S LESSON/THINGS WE LEARNED:

TODAY'S CAMPFIRE MENU:

Free Write:

Here is your chance to write what is on your mind, in your heart, or taking up space in your soul. Even if you don't think you have anything to write about today, take at least five minutes to free-form write whatever comes to mind. You might just be surprised!

DATE: ___ / ___ / ___

NAME: _____

OUR ADVENTURE BEGINS: _____

OUR POINT OF ORIGIN IS: _____

TODAY'S DESTINATION: _____

TODAY'S PASSENGER LOG:

_____
_____
_____
_____

WE SPENT THE NIGHT AT:

_____
_____

THE BEST PART OF THE DAY WAS:

_____
_____
_____
_____

TODAY'S LESSON/THINGS WE LEARNED:

_____
_____
_____
_____

TODAY'S CAMPFIRE MENU:

_____
_____
_____

A Letter to Pre-Van Life You:

Today's exercise is to explore how far you have come in your journeys. Take a few moments to write a letter to a past version of yourself to share all of the things you have learned so far. You can write to yourself as a child, as a teenager, or even take some time to share the fascinating things you've learned in just the past week.

At the end of the year, you'll be able to look back on all of the progress you have made as an individual, so don't be afraid to make note of both positive and negative experiences and emotions here.

_____
_____
_____
_____
_____
_____
_____
_____
_____
_____
_____
_____
_____
_____
_____
_____

DATE: ___ / ___ / ___

NAME: _____

OUR ADVENTURE BEGINS: _____

OUR POINT OF ORIGIN IS: _____

TODAY'S DESTINATION: _____

TODAY'S PASSENGER LOG:
_____
_____
_____
_____

WE SPENT THE NIGHT AT:
_____
_____

THE BEST PART OF THE DAY WAS:
_____
_____
_____
_____

TODAY'S LESSON/THINGS WE LEARNED:
_____
_____
_____
_____

TODAY'S CAMPFIRE MENU:

When we explore, we learn more. What is something new you have learned recently? From historical facts, to astronomical names, nothing is off limits. Divulge those new details!

DATE: ___ / ___ / ___

NAME: _____

OUR ADVENTURE BEGINS: _____

OUR POINT OF ORIGIN IS: _____

TODAY'S DESTINATION: _____

TODAY'S PASSENGER LOG:
_____
_____
_____
_____

WE SPENT THE NIGHT AT:
_____
_____

THE BEST PART OF THE DAY WAS:
_____
_____
_____
_____

TODAY'S LESSON/THINGS WE LEARNED:
_____
_____
_____
_____

TODAY'S CAMPFIRE MENU:

If you could have one thing from home right now, what would it be? On the other hand, what is something about van life that is far, far better on the road than it was at home?

DATE: ___ / ___ / ___

NAME: _____

OUR ADVENTURE BEGINS: _____

OUR POINT OF ORIGIN IS: _____

TODAY'S DESTINATION: _____

TODAY'S PASSENGER LOG:
_____
_____
_____
_____

WE SPENT THE NIGHT AT:
_____
_____

THE BEST PART OF THE DAY WAS:
_____
_____
_____
_____

TODAY'S LESSON/THINGS WE LEARNED:
_____
_____
_____
_____

TODAY'S CAMPFIRE MENU:

"We travel, some of us forever, to seek other places, other lives, other souls."
– Anais Nin

When you read this line, what comes to mind? Where are you in your adventure today? Reflect on this quote, and write your thoughts on how these words relate to your own journey.

DATE: ___ / ___ / ___

NAME: _____

OUR ADVENTURE BEGINS: _____

OUR POINT OF ORIGIN IS: _____

TODAY'S DESTINATION: _____

TODAY'S PASSENGER LOG:
_____
_____
_____
_____

WE SPENT THE NIGHT AT:
_____
_____

THE BEST PART OF THE DAY WAS:
_____
_____
_____
_____

TODAY'S LESSON/THINGS WE LEARNED:
_____
_____
_____
_____

TODAY'S CAMPFIRE MENU:

_____
_____
_____

Each week, allow yourself some time to pause to reflect on the past week, and to set the intention for the new week.

Where have you been in the past week- in your travels, in your daily life? How have you felt, mentally and physically? How do you intend to change this in the coming week?

_____
_____
_____
_____
_____
_____
_____
_____
_____
_____
_____
_____
_____
_____
_____
_____
_____
_____
_____
_____

DATE: ___ / ___ / ___

NAME:

OUR ADVENTURE BEGINS:

OUR POINT OF ORIGIN IS:

TODAY'S DESTINATION:

TODAY'S PASSENGER LOG:

WE SPENT THE NIGHT AT:

THE BEST PART OF THE DAY WAS:

TODAY'S LESSON/THINGS WE LEARNED:

TODAY'S CAMPFIRE MENU:

Today's writing prompt is a word. Take a few moments to meditate on this word, then write about how it relates to you and your adventures so far.

Belief

DATE: ___ / ___ / ___

NAME: _____

OUR ADVENTURE BEGINS: _____

OUR POINT OF ORIGIN IS: _____

TODAY'S DESTINATION: _____

TODAY'S PASSENGER LOG:
_____
_____
_____
_____

WE SPENT THE NIGHT AT:
_____
_____

THE BEST PART OF THE DAY WAS:
_____
_____
_____
_____

TODAY'S LESSON/THINGS WE LEARNED:
_____
_____
_____
_____

TODAY'S CAMPFIRE MENU:

Free Write:

Here is your chance to write what is on your mind, in your heart, or taking up space in your soul. Even if you don't think you have anything to write about today, take at least five minutes to free-form write whatever comes to mind. You might just be surprised!

DATE: ___ / ___ / ___

NAME: _____

OUR ADVENTURE BEGINS: _____

OUR POINT OF ORIGIN IS: _____

TODAY'S DESTINATION: _____

TODAY'S PASSENGER LOG:
_____
_____
_____
_____

WE SPENT THE NIGHT AT:
_____
_____

THE BEST PART OF THE DAY WAS:
_____
_____
_____
_____

TODAY'S LESSON/THINGS WE LEARNED:
_____
_____
_____
_____

TODAY'S CAMPFIRE MENU:

_____
_____
_____

A Letter to Pre-Van Life You:

Today's exercise is to explore how far you have come in your journeys. Take a few moments to write a letter to a past version of yourself to share all of the things you have learned so far. You can write to yourself as a child, as a teenager, or even take some time to share the fascinating things you've learned in just the past week.

At the end of the year, you'll be able to look back on all of the progress you have made as an individual, so don't be afraid to make note of both positive and negative experiences and emotions here.

_____
_____
_____
_____
_____
_____
_____
_____
_____
_____
_____
_____
_____
_____
_____
_____
_____
_____
_____

DATE: ___ / ___ / ___

NAME: _____

OUR ADVENTURE BEGINS: _____

OUR POINT OF ORIGIN IS: _____

TODAY'S DESTINATION: _____

TODAY'S PASSENGER LOG:
_____
_____
_____
_____

WE SPENT THE NIGHT AT:
_____
_____

THE BEST PART OF THE DAY WAS:
_____
_____
_____
_____

TODAY'S LESSON/THINGS WE LEARNED:
_____
_____
_____
_____

TODAY'S CAMPFIRE MENU:

Emotional check in! How have you been feeling? How do you feel right now? Any rough spots in the past few weeks? What about awesome moments? Make sure you're hydrated, rested, and bathed, then explore how you're feeling at this stage of your trip.

DATE: ___ / ___ / ___

NAME:

OUR ADVENTURE BEGINS:

OUR POINT OF ORIGIN IS:

TODAY'S DESTINATION:

TODAY'S PASSENGER LOG:

WE SPENT THE NIGHT AT:

THE BEST PART OF THE DAY WAS:

TODAY'S LESSON/THINGS WE LEARNED:

TODAY'S CAMPFIRE MENU:

Emotional check in! How have you been feeling? How do you feel right now? Any rough spots in the past few weeks? What about awesome moments? Make sure you're hydrated, rested, and bathed, then explore how you're feeling at this stage of your trip.

DATE: ___ / ___ / ___

NAME:

OUR ADVENTURE BEGINS:

OUR POINT OF ORIGIN IS:

TODAY'S DESTINATION:

TODAY'S PASSENGER LOG:

WE SPENT THE NIGHT AT:

THE BEST PART OF THE DAY WAS:

TODAY'S LESSON/THINGS WE LEARNED:

TODAY'S CAMPFIRE MENU:

*"Two roads diverged in a wood and I – I took the one less traveled by,
And that has made all the difference"*
– Robert Frost

When you read this line, what comes to mind? Where are you in your adventure today? Reflect on this quote, and write your thoughts on how these words relate to your own journey.

DATE: ___ / ___ / ___

NAME: _____

OUR ADVENTURE BEGINS: _____

OUR POINT OF ORIGIN IS: _____

TODAY'S DESTINATION: _____

TODAY'S PASSENGER LOG:

_____
_____
_____
_____

WE SPENT THE NIGHT AT:

_____
_____

THE BEST PART OF THE DAY WAS:

_____
_____
_____
_____

TODAY'S LESSON/THINGS WE LEARNED:

_____
_____
_____
_____

TODAY'S CAMPFIRE MENU:

Each week, allow yourself some time to pause to reflect on the past week, and to set the intention for the new week.

Where have you been in the past week- in your travels, in your daily life? How have you felt, mentally and physically? How do you intend to change this in the coming week?

DATE: ___ / ___ / ___

GOALS:

LOCATIONS VISITED:

THE TOP THREE MEMORIES:

1. _____
2. _____
3. _____

It's not healthy to keep those negative feelings bottled up, so let loose with the things that are frustrating you. Furthermore, how are you coping? What are some things that are helping you adjust? What are some things you should try? Try to work through your feelings here in order to set a new intention for positivity.

_____
_____
_____
_____
_____
_____
_____
_____
_____
_____
_____
_____
_____
_____
_____
_____
_____
_____

DATE: ___ / ___ / ___

NAME: _____

OUR ADVENTURE BEGINS: _____

OUR POINT OF ORIGIN IS: _____

TODAY'S DESTINATION: _____

TODAY'S PASSENGER LOG:

_____
_____
_____
_____

WE SPENT THE NIGHT AT:

_____
_____

THE BEST PART OF THE DAY WAS:

_____
_____
_____
_____

TODAY'S LESSON/THINGS WE LEARNED:

_____
_____
_____
_____

TODAY'S CAMPFIRE MENU:

Today's writing prompt is a word. Take a few moments to meditate on this word, then write about how it relates to you and your adventures so far.

Laugh

DATE: ___ / ___ / ___

NAME:

OUR ADVENTURE BEGINS:

OUR POINT OF ORIGIN IS:

TODAY'S DESTINATION:

TODAY'S PASSENGER LOG:

WE SPENT THE NIGHT AT:

THE BEST PART OF THE DAY WAS:

TODAY'S LESSON/THINGS WE LEARNED:

TODAY'S CAMPFIRE MENU:

Free Write:

Here is your chance to write what is on your mind, in your heart, or taking up space in your soul. Even if you don't think you have anything to write about today, take at least five minutes to free-form write whatever comes to mind. You might just be surprised!

DATE: ___ / ___ / ___

NAME: _____

OUR ADVENTURE BEGINS: _____

OUR POINT OF ORIGIN IS: _____

TODAY'S DESTINATION: _____

TODAY'S PASSENGER LOG:

_____
_____
_____
_____
_____

WE SPENT THE NIGHT AT:

_____
_____

THE BEST PART OF THE DAY WAS:

_____
_____
_____
_____

TODAY'S LESSON/THINGS WE LEARNED:

_____
_____
_____
_____

TODAY'S CAMPFIRE MENU:

_____
_____
_____

A Letter to Pre-Van Life You:

Today's exercise is to explore how far you have come in your journeys. Take a few moments to write a letter to a past version of yourself to share all of the things you have learned so far. You can write to yourself as a child, as a teenager, or even take some time to share the fascinating things you've learned in just the past week.

At the end of the year, you'll be able to look back on all of the progress you have made as an individual, so don't be afraid to make note of both positive and negative experiences and emotions here.

_____
_____
_____
_____
_____
_____
_____
_____
_____
_____
_____
_____
_____
_____
_____
_____
_____
_____

DATE: ___ / ___ / ___

NAME: _____

OUR ADVENTURE BEGINS: _____

OUR POINT OF ORIGIN IS: _____

TODAY'S DESTINATION: _____

TODAY'S PASSENGER LOG:
_____
_____
_____
_____

WE SPENT THE NIGHT AT:
_____
_____

THE BEST PART OF THE DAY WAS:
_____
_____
_____
_____

TODAY'S LESSON/THINGS WE LEARNED:
_____
_____
_____
_____

TODAY'S CAMPFIRE MENU:

Try something new today! Whether it's a new yoga pose, a different flavor of coffee, or exploring a National Park, do something out of the norm today.

DATE: ___ / ___ / ___

NAME: _____

OUR ADVENTURE BEGINS: _____

OUR POINT OF ORIGIN IS: _____

TODAY'S DESTINATION: _____

TODAY'S PASSENGER LOG:
_____
_____
_____
_____

WE SPENT THE NIGHT AT:
_____
_____

THE BEST PART OF THE DAY WAS:
_____
_____
_____
_____

TODAY'S LESSON/THINGS WE LEARNED:
_____
_____
_____
_____

TODAY'S CAMPFIRE MENU:

What's next? What are some things that you'd like to accomplish, now that you know you can make a go of this whole "van life" thing?

DATE: ___ / ___ / ___

NAME: _____

OUR ADVENTURE BEGINS: _____

OUR POINT OF ORIGIN IS: _____

TODAY'S DESTINATION: _____

TODAY'S PASSENGER LOG:
_____
_____
_____
_____

WE SPENT THE NIGHT AT:
_____
_____

THE BEST PART OF THE DAY WAS:
_____
_____
_____
_____

TODAY'S LESSON/THINGS WE LEARNED:
_____
_____
_____
_____

TODAY'S CAMPFIRE MENU:

"On the road of life, there are only two directions: the way you're going, and the way you've come."
— *Traditional*

When you read this line, what comes to mind? Where are you in your adventure today? Reflect on this quote, and write your thoughts on how these words relate to your own journey.

DATE: ___ / ___ / ___

NAME:

OUR ADVENTURE BEGINS:

OUR POINT OF ORIGIN IS:

TODAY'S DESTINATION:

TODAY'S PASSENGER LOG:

WE SPENT THE NIGHT AT:

THE BEST PART OF THE DAY WAS:

TODAY'S LESSON/THINGS WE LEARNED:

TODAY'S CAMPFIRE MENU:

Each week, allow yourself some time to pause to reflect on the past week, and to set the intention for the new week.

Where have you been in the past week- in your travels, in your daily life? How have you felt, mentally and physically? How do you intend to change this in the coming week?

DATE: ___ / ___ / ___

NAME: _____

OUR ADVENTURE BEGINS: _____

OUR POINT OF ORIGIN IS: _____

TODAY'S DESTINATION: _____

TODAY'S PASSENGER LOG:
_____
_____
_____
_____

WE SPENT THE NIGHT AT:
_____
_____

THE BEST PART OF THE DAY WAS:
_____
_____
_____
_____

TODAY'S LESSON/THINGS WE LEARNED:
_____
_____
_____
_____

TODAY'S CAMPFIRE MENU:

Today's writing prompt is a word. Take a few moments to meditate on this word, then write about how it relates to you and your adventures so far.

Opposites

DATE: ___ / ___ / ___

NAME: _____

OUR ADVENTURE BEGINS: _____

OUR POINT OF ORIGIN IS: _____

TODAY'S DESTINATION: _____

TODAY'S PASSENGER LOG:

_____
_____
_____
_____

WE SPENT THE NIGHT AT:

_____
_____

THE BEST PART OF THE DAY WAS:

_____
_____
_____
_____

TODAY'S LESSON/THINGS WE LEARNED:

_____
_____
_____
_____

TODAY'S CAMPFIRE MENU:

Free Write:

Here is your chance to write what is on your mind, in your heart, or taking up space in your soul. Even if you don't think you have anything to write about today, take at least five minutes to free-form write whatever comes to mind. You might just be surprised!

DATE: ___ / ___ / ___

NAME:

OUR ADVENTURE BEGINS:

OUR POINT OF ORIGIN IS:

TODAY'S DESTINATION:

TODAY'S PASSENGER LOG:

WE SPENT THE NIGHT AT:

THE BEST PART OF THE DAY WAS:

TODAY'S LESSON/THINGS WE LEARNED:

TODAY'S CAMPFIRE MENU:

A Letter to Pre-Van Life You:

Today's exercise is to explore how far you have come in your journeys. Take a few moments to write a letter to a past version of yourself to share all of the things you have learned so far. You can write to yourself as a child, as a teenager, or even take some time to share the fascinating things you've learned in just the past week.

At the end of the year, you'll be able to look back on all of the progress you have made as an individual, so don't be afraid to make note of both positive and negative experiences and emotions here.

DATE: ___ / ___ / ___

NAME: _____

OUR ADVENTURE BEGINS: _____

OUR POINT OF ORIGIN IS: _____

TODAY'S DESTINATION: _____

TODAY'S PASSENGER LOG:
_____
_____
_____
_____

WE SPENT THE NIGHT AT:
_____
_____

THE BEST PART OF THE DAY WAS:
_____
_____
_____
_____

TODAY'S LESSON/THINGS WE LEARNED:
_____
_____
_____
_____

TODAY'S CAMPFIRE MENU:

_____
_____
_____

How do you honestly feel about van life today? It's ok to have lots of different feelings, so use this time to explore your thoughts.

_____
_____
_____
_____
_____
_____
_____
_____
_____
_____
_____
_____
_____
_____
_____
_____
_____
_____
_____

DATE: ___ / ___ / ___

NAME: _____

OUR ADVENTURE BEGINS: _____

OUR POINT OF ORIGIN IS: _____

TODAY'S DESTINATION: _____

TODAY'S PASSENGER LOG:
_____
_____
_____
_____

WE SPENT THE NIGHT AT:
_____
_____

THE BEST PART OF THE DAY WAS:
_____
_____
_____
_____

TODAY'S LESSON/THINGS WE LEARNED:
_____
_____
_____
_____

TODAY'S CAMPFIRE MENU:

_____
_____
_____

Write about your worst day so far on this adventure. What went wrong? How did you feel? One day, you'll look back at this in a different light, so be sure to capture all of your thoughts and feelings.

DATE: ___ / ___ / ___

NAME: _____

OUR ADVENTURE BEGINS: _____

OUR POINT OF ORIGIN IS: _____

TODAY'S DESTINATION: _____

TODAY'S PASSENGER LOG:
_____
_____
_____
_____

WE SPENT THE NIGHT AT:
_____
_____

THE BEST PART OF THE DAY WAS:
_____
_____
_____
_____

TODAY'S LESSON/THINGS WE LEARNED:
_____
_____
_____
_____

TODAY'S CAMPFIRE MENU:

"Once in a while it really hits people that they don't have to experience the world in the way they have been told to."
– Alan Keightley

When you read this line, what comes to mind? Where are you in your adventure today? Reflect on this quote, and write your thoughts on how these words relate to your own journey.

DATE: ___ / ___ / ___

NAME: _____

OUR ADVENTURE BEGINS: _____

OUR POINT OF ORIGIN IS: _____

TODAY'S DESTINATION: _____

TODAY'S PASSENGER LOG:
_____
_____
_____
_____

WE SPENT THE NIGHT AT:
_____
_____

THE BEST PART OF THE DAY WAS:
_____
_____
_____
_____

TODAY'S LESSON/THINGS WE LEARNED:
_____
_____
_____
_____

TODAY'S CAMPFIRE MENU:

_____
_____
_____

Each week, allow yourself some time to pause to reflect on the past week, and to set the intention for the new week.

Where have you been in the past week- in your travels, in your daily life? How have you felt, mentally and physically? How do you intend to change this in the coming week?

_____
_____
_____
_____
_____
_____
_____
_____
_____
_____
_____
_____
_____
_____
_____
_____
_____
_____
_____
_____

DATE: ___ / ___ / ___

NAME:

OUR ADVENTURE BEGINS:

OUR POINT OF ORIGIN IS:

TODAY'S DESTINATION:

TODAY'S PASSENGER LOG:

WE SPENT THE NIGHT AT:

THE BEST PART OF THE DAY WAS:

TODAY'S LESSON/THINGS WE LEARNED:

TODAY'S CAMPFIRE MENU:

Today's writing prompt is a word. Take a few moments to meditate on this word, then write about how it relates to you and your adventures so far.

Unplanned

DATE: ___ / ___ / ___

NAME: _____

OUR ADVENTURE BEGINS: _____

OUR POINT OF ORIGIN IS: _____

TODAY'S DESTINATION: _____

TODAY'S PASSENGER LOG:
_____
_____
_____
_____

WE SPENT THE NIGHT AT:
_____
_____

THE BEST PART OF THE DAY WAS:
_____
_____
_____
_____

TODAY'S LESSON/THINGS WE LEARNED:
_____
_____
_____
_____

TODAY'S CAMPFIRE MENU:

_____
_____
_____

Free Write:

Here is your chance to write what is on your mind, in your heart, or taking up space in your soul. Even if you don't think you have anything to write about today, take at least five minutes to free-form write whatever comes to mind. You might just be surprised!

_____
_____
_____
_____
_____
_____
_____
_____
_____
_____
_____
_____
_____
_____
_____
_____
_____
_____
_____
_____
_____

DATE: ___ / ___ / ___

NAME: _____

OUR ADVENTURE BEGINS: _____

OUR POINT OF ORIGIN IS: _____

TODAY'S DESTINATION: _____

TODAY'S PASSENGER LOG:

_____
_____
_____
_____

WE SPENT THE NIGHT AT:

_____
_____

THE BEST PART OF THE DAY WAS:

_____
_____
_____
_____

TODAY'S LESSON/THINGS WE LEARNED:

_____
_____
_____
_____

TODAY'S CAMPFIRE MENU:

_____
_____
_____

A Letter to Pre-Van Life You:

Today's exercise is to explore how far you have come in your journeys. Take a few moments to write a letter to a past version of yourself to share all of the things you have learned so far. You can write to yourself as a child, as a teenager, or even take some time to share the fascinating things you've learned in just the past week.

At the end of the year, you'll be able to look back on all of the progress you have made as an individual, so don't be afraid to make note of both positive and negative experiences and emotions here.

DATE: ___ / ___ / ___

NAME: _____

OUR ADVENTURE BEGINS: _____

OUR POINT OF ORIGIN IS: _____

TODAY'S DESTINATION: _____

TODAY'S PASSENGER LOG:
_____
_____
_____
_____

WE SPENT THE NIGHT AT:
_____
_____

THE BEST PART OF THE DAY WAS:
_____
_____
_____
_____

TODAY'S LESSON/THINGS WE LEARNED:
_____
_____
_____
_____

TODAY'S CAMPFIRE MENU:

When we explore, we learn more. What is something new you have learned recently? From historical facts, to astronomical names, nothing is off limits. Divulge those new details!

DATE: ___ / ___ / ___

NAME: _____

OUR ADVENTURE BEGINS: _____

OUR POINT OF ORIGIN IS: _____

TODAY'S DESTINATION: _____

TODAY'S PASSENGER LOG:

_____
_____
_____
_____
_____

WE SPENT THE NIGHT AT:

_____
_____

THE BEST PART OF THE DAY WAS:

_____
_____
_____
_____

TODAY'S LESSON/THINGS WE LEARNED:

_____
_____
_____
_____

TODAY'S CAMPFIRE MENU:

If you could have one thing from home right now, what would it be? On the other hand, what is something about van life that is far, far better on the road than it was at home?

DATE: ___ / ___ / ___

NAME:

OUR ADVENTURE BEGINS:

OUR POINT OF ORIGIN IS:

TODAY'S DESTINATION:

TODAY'S PASSENGER LOG:

WE SPENT THE NIGHT AT:

THE BEST PART OF THE DAY WAS:

TODAY'S LESSON/THINGS WE LEARNED:

TODAY'S CAMPFIRE MENU:

"Travel makes one modest. You see what a tiny place you occupy in the world."
— Gustave Flaubert

When you read this line, what comes to mind? Where are you in your adventure today? Reflect on this quote, and write your thoughts on how these words relate to your own journey.

DATE: ___ / ___ / ___

NAME: _____

OUR ADVENTURE BEGINS: _____

OUR POINT OF ORIGIN IS: _____

TODAY'S DESTINATION: _____

TODAY'S PASSENGER LOG:

_____
_____
_____
_____

WE SPENT THE NIGHT AT:

_____
_____

THE BEST PART OF THE DAY WAS:

_____
_____
_____
_____

TODAY'S LESSON/THINGS WE LEARNED:

_____
_____
_____
_____

TODAY'S CAMPFIRE MENU:

_____
_____
_____

Each week, allow yourself some time to pause to reflect on the past week, and to set the intention for the new week.

Where have you been in the past week- in your travels, in your daily life? How have you felt, mentally and physically? How do you intend to change this in the coming week?

_____
_____
_____
_____
_____
_____
_____
_____
_____
_____
_____
_____
_____
_____
_____
_____
_____
_____
_____
_____
_____

DATE: ___ / ___ / ___

NAME: _____

OUR ADVENTURE BEGINS: _____

OUR POINT OF ORIGIN IS: _____

TODAY'S DESTINATION: _____

TODAY'S PASSENGER LOG:
_____
_____
_____
_____

WE SPENT THE NIGHT AT:
_____
_____

THE BEST PART OF THE DAY WAS:
_____
_____
_____
_____

TODAY'S LESSON/THINGS WE LEARNED:
_____
_____
_____
_____

TODAY'S CAMPFIRE MENU:

Today's writing prompt is a word. Take a few moments to meditate on this word, then write about how it relates to you and your adventures so far.

Expectations

DATE: ___ / ___ / ___

NAME: _____

OUR ADVENTURE BEGINS: _____

OUR POINT OF ORIGIN IS: _____

TODAY'S DESTINATION: _____

TODAY'S PASSENGER LOG:

_____
_____
_____
_____
_____

WE SPENT THE NIGHT AT:

_____
_____

THE BEST PART OF THE DAY WAS:

_____
_____
_____
_____

TODAY'S LESSON/THINGS WE LEARNED:

_____
_____
_____
_____

TODAY'S CAMPFIRE MENU:

Free Write:

Here is your chance to write what is on your mind, in your heart, or taking up space in your soul. Even if you don't think you have anything to write about today, take at least five minutes to free-form write whatever comes to mind. You might just be surprised!

DATE: ___ / ___ / ___

NAME: _____

OUR ADVENTURE BEGINS: _____

OUR POINT OF ORIGIN IS: _____

TODAY'S DESTINATION: _____

TODAY'S PASSENGER LOG:
_____
_____
_____
_____

WE SPENT THE NIGHT AT:
_____
_____

THE BEST PART OF THE DAY WAS:
_____
_____
_____
_____

TODAY'S LESSON/THINGS WE LEARNED:
_____
_____
_____
_____

TODAY'S CAMPFIRE MENU:

A Letter to Pre-Van Life You:

Today's exercise is to explore how far you have come in your journeys. Take a few moments to write a letter to a past version of yourself to share all of the things you have learned so far. You can write to yourself as a child, as a teenager, or even take some time to share the fascinating things you've learned in just the past week.

At the end of the year, you'll be able to look back on all of the progress you have made as an individual, so don't be afraid to make note of both positive and negative experiences and emotions here.

DATE: ___ / ___ / ___

NAME: _____

OUR ADVENTURE BEGINS: _____

OUR POINT OF ORIGIN IS: _____

TODAY'S DESTINATION: _____

TODAY'S PASSENGER LOG:
_____
_____
_____
_____

WE SPENT THE NIGHT AT:
_____
_____

THE BEST PART OF THE DAY WAS:
_____
_____
_____
_____

TODAY'S LESSON/THINGS WE LEARNED:
_____
_____
_____
_____

TODAY'S CAMPFIRE MENU:

Emotional check in! How have you been feeling? How do you feel right now? Any rough spots in the past few weeks? What about awesome moments? Make sure you're hydrated, rested, and bathed, then explore how you're feeling at this stage of your trip.

DATE: ___ / ___ / ___

NAME:

OUR ADVENTURE BEGINS:

OUR POINT OF ORIGIN IS:

TODAY'S DESTINATION:

TODAY'S PASSENGER LOG:

WE SPENT THE NIGHT AT:

THE BEST PART OF THE DAY WAS:

TODAY'S LESSON/THINGS WE LEARNED:

TODAY'S CAMPFIRE MENU:

Emotional check in! How have you been feeling? How do you feel right now? Any rough spots in the past few weeks? What about awesome moments? Make sure you're hydrated, rested, and bathed, then explore how you're feeling at this stage of your trip.

DATE: ___ / ___ / ___

NAME:

OUR ADVENTURE BEGINS:

OUR POINT OF ORIGIN IS:

TODAY'S DESTINATION:

TODAY'S PASSENGER LOG:

WE SPENT THE NIGHT AT:

THE BEST PART OF THE DAY WAS:

TODAY'S LESSON/THINGS WE LEARNED:

TODAY'S CAMPFIRE MENU:

"The journey is part of the experience — an expression of the seriousness of one's intent. One doesn't take the A train to Mecca."
– Anthony Bourdain

When you read this line, what comes to mind? Where are you in your adventure today? Reflect on this quote, and write your thoughts on how these words relate to your own journey.

DATE: ___ / ___ / ___

NAME: _____

OUR ADVENTURE BEGINS: _____

OUR POINT OF ORIGIN IS: _____

TODAY'S DESTINATION: _____

TODAY'S PASSENGER LOG:
_____
_____
_____
_____

WE SPENT THE NIGHT AT:
_____
_____

THE BEST PART OF THE DAY WAS:
_____
_____
_____
_____

TODAY'S LESSON/THINGS WE LEARNED:
_____
_____
_____
_____

TODAY'S CAMPFIRE MENU:

Each week, allow yourself some time to pause to reflect on the past week, and to set the intention for the new week.

Where have you been in the past week- in your travels, in your daily life? How have you felt, mentally and physically? How do you intend to change this in the coming week?

DATE: ____ / ____ / ____

GOALS:
_____
_____
_____
_____
_____

LOCATIONS VISITED:
_____
_____
_____
_____
_____

THE TOP THREE MEMORIES:

1. _____
2. _____
3. _____

Setting goals can be scary, especially if they're particularly difficult to achieve or have a very tight deadline. But what if you were to set some intentions for things to accomplish this year? What are some dreams that you haven't visited yet? Don't worry about making plans, just think about things you'd like to do someday. No pressure!

_____
_____
_____
_____
_____
_____
_____
_____
_____
_____
_____
_____
_____
_____
_____
_____
_____
_____
_____
_____

DATE: ___ / ___ / ___

NAME: _____

OUR ADVENTURE BEGINS: _____

OUR POINT OF ORIGIN IS: _____

TODAY'S DESTINATION: _____

TODAY'S PASSENGER LOG:
_____
_____
_____
_____
_____

WE SPENT THE NIGHT AT:
_____
_____

THE BEST PART OF THE DAY WAS:
_____
_____
_____
_____

TODAY'S LESSON/THINGS WE LEARNED:
_____
_____
_____
_____

TODAY'S CAMPFIRE MENU:

Today's writing prompt is a word. Take a few moments to meditate on this word, then write about how it relates to you and your adventures so far.

Flexibility

DATE: ___ / ___ / ___

NAME: _____

OUR ADVENTURE BEGINS: _____

OUR POINT OF ORIGIN IS: _____

TODAY'S DESTINATION: _____

TODAY'S PASSENGER LOG:

_____
_____
_____
_____

WE SPENT THE NIGHT AT:

_____
_____

THE BEST PART OF THE DAY WAS:

_____
_____
_____
_____

TODAY'S LESSON/THINGS WE LEARNED:

_____
_____
_____
_____

TODAY'S CAMPFIRE MENU:

Free Write:

Here is your chance to write what is on your mind, in your heart, or taking up space in your soul. Even if you don't think you have anything to write about today, take at least five minutes to free-form write whatever comes to mind. You might just be surprised!

DATE: ___ / ___ / ___

NAME: _____

OUR ADVENTURE BEGINS: _____

OUR POINT OF ORIGIN IS: _____

TODAY'S DESTINATION: _____

TODAY'S PASSENGER LOG:

_____
_____
_____
_____

WE SPENT THE NIGHT AT:

_____
_____

THE BEST PART OF THE DAY WAS:

_____
_____
_____
_____

TODAY'S LESSON/THINGS WE LEARNED:

_____
_____
_____
_____

TODAY'S CAMPFIRE MENU:

A Letter to Pre-Van Life You:

Today's exercise is to explore how far you have come in your journeys. Take a few moments to write a letter to a past version of yourself to share all of the things you have learned so far. You can write to yourself as a child, as a teenager, or even take some time to share the fascinating things you've learned in just the past week.

At the end of the year, you'll be able to look back on all of the progress you have made as an individual, so don't be afraid to make note of both positive and negative experiences and emotions here.

DATE: ___ / ___ / ___

NAME:

OUR ADVENTURE BEGINS:

OUR POINT OF ORIGIN IS:

TODAY'S DESTINATION:

TODAY'S PASSENGER LOG:

WE SPENT THE NIGHT AT:

THE BEST PART OF THE DAY WAS:

TODAY'S LESSON/THINGS WE LEARNED:

TODAY'S CAMPFIRE MENU:

Try something new today! Whether it's a new yoga pose, a different flavor of coffee, or exploring a National Park, do something out of the norm today.

DATE: ___ / ___ / ___

NAME: _____

OUR ADVENTURE BEGINS: _____

OUR POINT OF ORIGIN IS: _____

TODAY'S DESTINATION: _____

TODAY'S PASSENGER LOG:

_____
_____
_____
_____

WE SPENT THE NIGHT AT:

_____
_____

THE BEST PART OF THE DAY WAS:

_____
_____
_____
_____

TODAY'S LESSON/THINGS WE LEARNED:

_____
_____
_____
_____

TODAY'S CAMPFIRE MENU:

_____
_____
_____

What's next? What are some things that you'd like to accomplish, now that you know you can make a go of this whole "van life" thing?

_____
_____
_____
_____
_____
_____
_____
_____
_____
_____
_____
_____
_____
_____
_____
_____
_____
_____
_____

DATE: ____ / ____ / ____

NAME: _____

OUR ADVENTURE BEGINS: _____

OUR POINT OF ORIGIN IS: _____

TODAY'S DESTINATION: _____

TODAY'S PASSENGER LOG:

_____
_____
_____
_____

WE SPENT THE NIGHT AT:

_____
_____

THE BEST PART OF THE DAY WAS:

_____
_____
_____
_____

TODAY'S LESSON/THINGS WE LEARNED:

_____
_____
_____
_____

TODAY'S CAMPFIRE MENU:

_____
_____
_____

"Not all those who wander are lost."
– J.R.R. Tolkien

When you read this line, what comes to mind? Where are you in your adventure today? Reflect on this quote, and write your thoughts on how these words relate to your own journey.

_____
_____
_____
_____
_____
_____
_____
_____
_____
_____
_____
_____
_____
_____
_____
_____
_____
_____
_____
_____
_____

DATE: ___ / ___ / ___

NAME: _____

OUR ADVENTURE BEGINS: _____

OUR POINT OF ORIGIN IS: _____

TODAY'S DESTINATION: _____

TODAY'S PASSENGER LOG:
_____
_____
_____
_____

WE SPENT THE NIGHT AT:
_____
_____

THE BEST PART OF THE DAY WAS:
_____
_____
_____
_____

TODAY'S LESSON/THINGS WE LEARNED:
_____
_____
_____
_____

TODAY'S CAMPFIRE MENU:

Each week, allow yourself some time to pause to reflect on the past week, and to set the intention for the new week.

Where have you been in the past week- in your travels, in your daily life? How have you felt, mentally and physically? How do you intend to change this in the coming week?

DATE: ___ / ___ / ___

NAME: _____

OUR ADVENTURE BEGINS: _____

OUR POINT OF ORIGIN IS: _____

TODAY'S DESTINATION: _____

TODAY'S PASSENGER LOG:
_____
_____
_____
_____

WE SPENT THE NIGHT AT:
_____
_____

THE BEST PART OF THE DAY WAS:
_____
_____
_____
_____

TODAY'S LESSON/THINGS WE LEARNED:
_____
_____
_____
_____

TODAY'S CAMPFIRE MENU:

Today's writing prompt is a word. Take a few moments to meditate on this word, then write about how it relates to you and your adventures so far.

Alive

DATE: ___ / ___ / ___

NAME: _____

OUR ADVENTURE BEGINS: _____

OUR POINT OF ORIGIN IS: _____

TODAY'S DESTINATION: _____

TODAY'S PASSENGER LOG:
_____
_____
_____
_____

WE SPENT THE NIGHT AT:
_____
_____

THE BEST PART OF THE DAY WAS:
_____
_____
_____
_____

TODAY'S LESSON/THINGS WE LEARNED:
_____
_____
_____
_____

TODAY'S CAMPFIRE MENU:

Free Write:

Here is your chance to write what is on your mind, in your heart, or taking up space in your soul. Even if you don't think you have anything to write about today, take at least five minutes to free-form write whatever comes to mind. You might just be surprised!

DATE: ___ / ___ / ___

NAME: _____

OUR ADVENTURE BEGINS: _____

OUR POINT OF ORIGIN IS: _____

TODAY'S DESTINATION: _____

TODAY'S PASSENGER LOG:
_____
_____
_____
_____

WE SPENT THE NIGHT AT:
_____
_____

THE BEST PART OF THE DAY WAS:
_____
_____
_____
_____

TODAY'S LESSON/THINGS WE LEARNED:
_____
_____
_____
_____

TODAY'S CAMPFIRE MENU:

_____
_____
_____

A Letter to Pre-Van Life You:

Today's exercise is to explore how far you have come in your journeys. Take a few moments to write a letter to a past version of yourself to share all of the things you have learned so far. You can write to yourself as a child, as a teenager, or even take some time to share the fascinating things you've learned in just the past week.

At the end of the year, you'll be able to look back on all of the progress you have made as an individual, so don't be afraid to make note of both positive and negative experiences and emotions here.

_____
_____
_____
_____
_____
_____
_____
_____
_____
_____
_____
_____
_____
_____
_____
_____
_____
_____
_____

DATE: ___ / ___ / ___

NAME: _____

OUR ADVENTURE BEGINS: _____

OUR POINT OF ORIGIN IS: _____

TODAY'S DESTINATION: _____

TODAY'S PASSENGER LOG:

_____
_____
_____
_____

WE SPENT THE NIGHT AT:

_____
_____

THE BEST PART OF THE DAY WAS:

_____
_____
_____
_____

TODAY'S LESSON/THINGS WE LEARNED:

_____
_____
_____
_____

TODAY'S CAMPFIRE MENU:

How do you honestly feel about van life today? It's ok to have lots of different feelings, so use this time to explore your thoughts.

DATE: ___ / ___ / ___

NAME: _____

OUR ADVENTURE BEGINS: _____

OUR POINT OF ORIGIN IS: _____

TODAY'S DESTINATION: _____

TODAY'S PASSENGER LOG:

_____
_____
_____
_____

WE SPENT THE NIGHT AT:

_____
_____

THE BEST PART OF THE DAY WAS:

_____
_____
_____
_____

TODAY'S LESSON/THINGS WE LEARNED:

_____
_____
_____
_____

TODAY'S CAMPFIRE MENU:

Write about your worst day so far on this adventure. What went wrong? How did you feel? One day, you'll look back at this in a different light, so be sure to capture all of your thoughts and feelings.

DATE: ___ / ___ / ___

NAME: _____

OUR ADVENTURE BEGINS: _____

OUR POINT OF ORIGIN IS: _____

TODAY'S DESTINATION: _____

TODAY'S PASSENGER LOG:
_____
_____
_____
_____

WE SPENT THE NIGHT AT:
_____
_____

THE BEST PART OF THE DAY WAS:
_____
_____
_____
_____

TODAY'S LESSON/THINGS WE LEARNED:
_____
_____
_____
_____

TODAY'S CAMPFIRE MENU:

"The life you have led doesn't need to be the only life you have."
– Anna Quindlen

When you read this line, what comes to mind? Where are you in your adventure today? Reflect on this quote, and write your thoughts on how these words relate to your own journey.

DATE: ___ / ___ / ___

NAME: _____

OUR ADVENTURE BEGINS: _____

OUR POINT OF ORIGIN IS: _____

TODAY'S DESTINATION: _____

TODAY'S PASSENGER LOG:

_____
_____
_____
_____

WE SPENT THE NIGHT AT:

_____
_____

THE BEST PART OF THE DAY WAS:

_____
_____
_____
_____

TODAY'S LESSON/THINGS WE LEARNED:

_____
_____
_____
_____

TODAY'S CAMPFIRE MENU:

_____
_____
_____

Each week, allow yourself some time to pause to reflect on the past week, and to set the intention for the new week.

Where have you been in the past week- in your travels, in your daily life? How have you felt, mentally and physically? How do you intend to change this in the coming week?

DATE: ___ / ___ / ___

NAME: _____

OUR ADVENTURE BEGINS: _____

OUR POINT OF ORIGIN IS: _____

TODAY'S DESTINATION: _____

TODAY'S PASSENGER LOG:

_____
_____
_____
_____

WE SPENT THE NIGHT AT:

_____
_____

THE BEST PART OF THE DAY WAS:

_____
_____
_____
_____

TODAY'S LESSON/THINGS WE LEARNED:

_____
_____
_____
_____

TODAY'S CAMPFIRE MENU:

Today's writing prompt is a word. Take a few moments to meditate on this word, then write about how it relates to you and your adventures so far.

Grounding

DATE: ___ / ___ / ___

NAME: _____

OUR ADVENTURE BEGINS: _____

OUR POINT OF ORIGIN IS: _____

TODAY'S DESTINATION: _____

TODAY'S PASSENGER LOG:

_____
_____
_____
_____

WE SPENT THE NIGHT AT:

_____
_____

THE BEST PART OF THE DAY WAS:

_____
_____
_____
_____

TODAY'S LESSON/THINGS WE LEARNED:

_____
_____
_____
_____

TODAY'S CAMPFIRE MENU:

Free Write:

Here is your chance to write what is on your mind, in your heart, or taking up space in your soul. Even if you don't think you have anything to write about today, take at least five minutes to free-form write whatever comes to mind. You might just be surprised!

DATE: ___ / ___ / ___

NAME: _____

OUR ADVENTURE BEGINS: _____

OUR POINT OF ORIGIN IS: _____

TODAY'S DESTINATION: _____

TODAY'S PASSENGER LOG:

_____
_____
_____
_____

WE SPENT THE NIGHT AT:

_____
_____

THE BEST PART OF THE DAY WAS:

_____
_____
_____
_____

TODAY'S LESSON/THINGS WE LEARNED:

_____
_____
_____
_____

TODAY'S CAMPFIRE MENU:

_____
_____
_____

A Letter to Pre-Van Life You:

Today's exercise is to explore how far you have come in your journeys. Take a few moments to write a letter to a past version of yourself to share all of the things you have learned so far. You can write to yourself as a child, as a teenager, or even take some time to share the fascinating things you've learned in just the past week.

At the end of the year, you'll be able to look back on all of the progress you have made as an individual, so don't be afraid to make note of both positive and negative experiences and emotions here.

_____
_____
_____
_____
_____
_____
_____
_____
_____
_____
_____
_____
_____
_____
_____
_____
_____

DATE: ___ / ___ / ___

NAME: _____

OUR ADVENTURE BEGINS: _____

OUR POINT OF ORIGIN IS: _____

TODAY'S DESTINATION: _____

TODAY'S PASSENGER LOG:
_____
_____
_____
_____

WE SPENT THE NIGHT AT:
_____
_____

THE BEST PART OF THE DAY WAS:
_____
_____
_____
_____

TODAY'S LESSON/THINGS WE LEARNED:
_____
_____
_____
_____

TODAY'S CAMPFIRE MENU:

When we explore, we learn more. What is something new you have learned recently? From historical facts, to astronomical names, nothing is off limits. Divulge those new details!

DATE: ___ / ___ / ___

NAME: _____

OUR ADVENTURE BEGINS: _____

OUR POINT OF ORIGIN IS: _____

TODAY'S DESTINATION: _____

TODAY'S PASSENGER LOG:
_____
_____
_____
_____
_____

WE SPENT THE NIGHT AT:
_____
_____

THE BEST PART OF THE DAY WAS:
_____
_____
_____
_____

TODAY'S LESSON/THINGS WE LEARNED:
_____
_____
_____
_____

TODAY'S CAMPFIRE MENU:

If you could have one thing from home right now, what would it be? On the other hand, what is something about van life that is far, far better on the road than it was at home?

DATE: ____ / ____ / ____

NAME: _____

OUR ADVENTURE BEGINS: _____

OUR POINT OF ORIGIN IS: _____

TODAY'S DESTINATION: _____

TODAY'S PASSENGER LOG:

_____
_____
_____
_____

WE SPENT THE NIGHT AT:

_____
_____

THE BEST PART OF THE DAY WAS:

_____
_____
_____
_____

TODAY'S LESSON/THINGS WE LEARNED:

_____
_____
_____
_____

TODAY'S CAMPFIRE MENU:

_____

_____

_____

"The world is a book, and those who do not travel read only one page."
— Saint Augustine

When you read this line, what comes to mind? Where are you in your adventure today? Reflect on this quote, and write your thoughts on how these words relate to your own journey.

_____
_____
_____
_____
_____
_____
_____
_____
_____
_____
_____
_____
_____
_____
_____
_____
_____
_____
_____
_____

DATE: _____ / _____ / _____

NAME: _____

OUR ADVENTURE BEGINS: _____

OUR POINT OF ORIGIN IS: _____

TODAY'S DESTINATION: _____

TODAY'S PASSENGER LOG:

_____
_____
_____
_____

WE SPENT THE NIGHT AT:

_____
_____

THE BEST PART OF THE DAY WAS:

_____
_____
_____
_____

TODAY'S LESSON/THINGS WE LEARNED:

_____
_____
_____
_____

TODAY'S CAMPFIRE MENU:

Each week, allow yourself some time to pause to reflect on the past week, and to set the intention for the new week.

Where have you been in the past week- in your travels, in your daily life? How have you felt, mentally and physically? How do you intend to change this in the coming week?

DATE: ___ / ___ / ___

NAME:

OUR ADVENTURE BEGINS:

OUR POINT OF ORIGIN IS:

TODAY'S DESTINATION:

TODAY'S PASSENGER LOG:

WE SPENT THE NIGHT AT:

THE BEST PART OF THE DAY WAS:

TODAY'S LESSON/THINGS WE LEARNED:

TODAY'S CAMPFIRE MENU:

Today's writing prompt is a word. Take a few moments to meditate on this word, then write about how it relates to you and your adventures so far.

Connection

DATE: ___ / ___ / ___

NAME: _____

OUR ADVENTURE BEGINS: _____

OUR POINT OF ORIGIN IS: _____

TODAY'S DESTINATION: _____

TODAY'S PASSENGER LOG:

_____
_____
_____
_____

WE SPENT THE NIGHT AT:

_____
_____

THE BEST PART OF THE DAY WAS:

_____
_____
_____
_____

TODAY'S LESSON/THINGS WE LEARNED:

_____
_____
_____
_____

TODAY'S CAMPFIRE MENU:

Free Write:

Here is your chance to write what is on your mind, in your heart, or taking up space in your soul. Even if you don't think you have anything to write about today, take at least five minutes to free-form write whatever comes to mind. You might just be surprised!

DATE: ___ / ___ / ___

NAME: _____

OUR ADVENTURE BEGINS: _____

OUR POINT OF ORIGIN IS: _____

TODAY'S DESTINATION: _____

TODAY'S PASSENGER LOG:
_____
_____
_____
_____

WE SPENT THE NIGHT AT:
_____
_____

THE BEST PART OF THE DAY WAS:
_____
_____
_____
_____

TODAY'S LESSON/THINGS WE LEARNED:
_____
_____
_____
_____

TODAY'S CAMPFIRE MENU:

_____
_____
_____

A Letter to Pre-Van Life You:

Today's exercise is to explore how far you have come in your journeys. Take a few moments to write a letter to a past version of yourself to share all of the things you have learned so far. You can write to yourself as a child, as a teenager, or even take some time to share the fascinating things you've learned in just the past week.

At the end of the year, you'll be able to look back on all of the progress you have made as an individual, so don't be afraid to make note of both positive and negative experiences and emotions here.

_____
_____
_____
_____
_____
_____
_____
_____
_____
_____
_____
_____
_____
_____
_____
_____
_____
_____
_____
_____

DATE: ___ / ___ / ___

NAME:

OUR ADVENTURE BEGINS:

OUR POINT OF ORIGIN IS:

TODAY'S DESTINATION:

TODAY'S PASSENGER LOG:

WE SPENT THE NIGHT AT:

THE BEST PART OF THE DAY WAS:

TODAY'S LESSON/THINGS WE LEARNED:

TODAY'S CAMPFIRE MENU:

Emotional check in! How have you been feeling? How do you feel right now? Any rough spots in the past few weeks? What about awesome moments? Make sure you're hydrated, rested, and bathed, then explore how you're feeling at this stage of your trip.

DATE: ___ / ___ / ___

NAME: _____

OUR ADVENTURE BEGINS: _____

OUR POINT OF ORIGIN IS: _____

TODAY'S DESTINATION: _____

TODAY'S PASSENGER LOG:

_____
_____
_____
_____

WE SPENT THE NIGHT AT:

_____
_____

THE BEST PART OF THE DAY WAS:

_____
_____
_____
_____

TODAY'S LESSON/THINGS WE LEARNED:

_____
_____
_____
_____

TODAY'S CAMPFIRE MENU:

Emotional check in! How have you been feeling? How do you feel right now? Any rough spots in the past few weeks? What about awesome moments? Make sure you're hydrated, rested, and bathed, then explore how you're feeling at this stage of your trip.

DATE: ___ / ___ / ___

NAME: _____

OUR ADVENTURE BEGINS: _____

OUR POINT OF ORIGIN IS: _____

TODAY'S DESTINATION: _____

TODAY'S PASSENGER LOG:
_____
_____
_____
_____

WE SPENT THE NIGHT AT:
_____
_____

THE BEST PART OF THE DAY WAS:
_____
_____
_____
_____

TODAY'S LESSON/THINGS WE LEARNED:
_____
_____
_____
_____

TODAY'S CAMPFIRE MENU:

_____

_____

"Travel is the only thing you buy that makes you richer."
– Anonymous

When you read this line, what comes to mind? Where are you in your adventure today? Reflect on this quote, and write your thoughts on how these words relate to your own journey.

_____

_____

_____

_____

_____

_____

_____

_____

_____

_____

_____

_____

_____

_____

_____

_____

_____

_____

DATE: ___ / ___ / ___

NAME: _____

OUR ADVENTURE BEGINS: _____

OUR POINT OF ORIGIN IS: _____

TODAY'S DESTINATION: _____

TODAY'S PASSENGER LOG:
_____
_____
_____
_____

WE SPENT THE NIGHT AT:
_____
_____

THE BEST PART OF THE DAY WAS:
_____
_____
_____
_____

TODAY'S LESSON/THINGS WE LEARNED:
_____
_____
_____
_____

TODAY'S CAMPFIRE MENU:

_____
_____
_____

Each week, allow yourself some time to pause to reflect on the past week, and to set the intention for the new week.

Where have you been in the past week- in your travels, in your daily life? How have you felt, mentally and physically? How do you intend to change this in the coming week?

_____
_____
_____
_____
_____
_____
_____
_____
_____
_____
_____
_____
_____
_____
_____
_____
_____
_____
_____
_____

For your inspiration take a look at these books

How to Choose the Ultimate Side-hustle

mybook.to/side-hustle

Things Every Lifer Needs to Know

mybook.to/vanlife

Finding Success Outside The Traditional Office

mybook.to/workfromanywhere

From Wheels to Wellness

mybook.to/Healthinvan

www.ingramcontent.com/pod-product-compliance
Lightning Source LLC
Chambersburg PA
CBHW081306070526
44578CB00006B/817